WAKEFIELD

**libraries**
& information services

**Schools Library Service**

**SCHOOL LIBRARY SERVICE
LIBRARY HEADQUARTERS
BALNE LANE.
WAKEFIELD. WF2 0DQ**

Tel. 01924 302238/
302239

Featurenet 850
2238/2239

WHO WAS...

# JOHN LENNON

## The Beatle with the Big Mouth

### LIZ GOGERLY

Illustrations by Alex Fox

**✳ SHORT BOOKS**

First published in 2005 by

Short Books

15 Highbury Terrace

London N5 1UP


10 9 8 7 6 5 4 3 2 1

A CIP catalogue record for this book
is available from the British Library.


Illustration copyright © Alex Fox 2005

Quiz by Sebastian Blake


ISBN 1-904977-14-6


Printed in Great Britain by
Bookmarque Ltd., Croydon, Surrey

For Johnny – my own beautiful boy

# CHAPTER 1

On 25 March, 1969, John Lennon and Yoko Ono invited the world's press to their honeymoon. Five days earlier the couple had married in Gibraltar. They had worn all-white clothes, including white socks and tennis shoes. Yoko's black eyes had twinkled with joy under her large floppy white hat. John had held onto her tiny hand with pride. The newspapers splashed photographs of the smiling Beatle and his new wife on their front covers. What, pondered the news hounds, would the crazy couple do next?

When an invitation to meet John and Yoko had plopped on to the desks of various press offices and newsrooms around the globe there had been a flurry of excitement. Why would John Lennon, the most outspoken member of the Beatles, want a bunch of reporters to meet him in his bedroom while he was on his honeymoon? Surely, the newly weds wanted to be alone to get on with whatever newly-weds did? Even with these questions rattling around their heads the journalists lost little time in accepting the curious invitation. After all, any headline with John Lennon in it was well worth pursuing.

Meanwhile, John and Yoko had taken up residence in the presidential suite of the Amsterdam Hilton, one of the swankiest hotels in the Dutch capital.

'This is so exciting,' chirped Yoko as she gazed around the posh room. 'Seven days and nights – just you and me and the world's press.'

'Best of all,' laughed John, 'We're going to spend the whole time in bed!'

'Yeah,' mused Yoko. 'That'll give them something to talk about.' And they both started to giggle.

The first journalists to arrive in John and Yoko's room were astounded by what they saw. The kooky couple were propped up in bed looking as calm and relaxed as two smug pussycats who'd had cream for breakfast, lunch and supper. They were both wearing white pyjamas – wow, at least they had had the decency to cover up because there had been talk that they might be naked! Their long dark hair flowed over their shoulders – some of the journalists thought John could do with a sensible haircut. Above their heads were two handwritten signs reading: 'Bed Peace' and 'Hair Peace'. The room was strewn with so many flowers it was like stepping into a florist's shop.

Typically, John couldn't keep quiet for long – he was bursting to tell the journalists why he'd invited them.

'These days I can't even buy a can a baked beans

without somebody from the press being there to report on it,' he told them in his flat nasal voice. 'Let's face it guys, you'd have been on our honeymoon whether we'd invited you or not!'

The journalists were taken aback, but he always was the Beatle with the big mouth.

'We're going to do something worthwhile with our fame,' John explained. 'It's one thing being a Beatle. But I want to show you all that John Lennon stands for peace.' John's face beamed.

'And, Yoko and I are going to stay in this big bed just to tell you what we think about peace and the mess we're making of the world with war and violence. What's so wrong with love, peace and understanding eh?'

In the seven days of the famous 'Bed-in for Peace' over one hundred journalists trooped up to room 902 of the Amsterdam Hilton to hear John and Yoko talk. Since the 1950s a terrible war had been raging in Vietnam and thousands of innocent Vietnamese civilians and soldiers had been killed. In the 1960s thousands of young American servicemen had also died or gone missing in Vietnam.

'All war is a senseless loss of life,' John told the journalists.

'What's happening in Vietnam is criminal. There are ordinary women and children dying. And for what? Nothing.' There was an angry glint in his eyes now. 'I was born during the Second World War. I know I didn't suffer like those poor kids in Vietnam but we had it bad sometimes. Others kids at school lost fathers, brothers or uncles in the war. We all had rationing. Sometimes we had to make do on next to nothing. Things were pretty grim for a while. In the end what did that war achieve except misery and heartache?'

John went on to talk about the German leader Adolf Hitler who had started the Second World War. And, he talked about religion and Jesus Christ: 'We want Christ to win,' he told the stunned journalists.

Most of the media thought John and Yoko were mad and the bed-in was a joke.

'Hmmph, what a clown,' said one of the Fleet Street journalists. 'Does he really think he can achieve anything by wafting about in white and spreading petals everywhere?'

John said he didn't mind being a 'clown' if it helped to spread a message of peace. And, for a while, the bed-in did make people stop and think. Many Beatles fans thought John was a hero for speaking out against war. But many old people thought he was a troublemaker and the whole thing was ludicrous. This was the way it had always been with John – people either loved him or hated him.

# CHAPTER 2

In one of their most famous songs the Beatles told us that all we need is love. As a little boy, growing up in the rough, tough city of Liverpool, all John Lennon wanted was love.

John's mother Julia was a pretty auburn-haired woman who played the banjo and enjoyed a joke. His father, Freddy, was a sailor who shared Julia's colourful sense of humour. When John was born, on 9 October 1940, Freddy was away at sea so it was Julia's sister Mimi – solid, dependable, no-nonsense Mimi – who rushed to the Oxford Street Maternity Hospital to see the new baby.

'My, he's beautiful,' Mimi told Julia, whose face was red and glowing with pride.

'He's not wrinkled like the other babies,' Mimi gushed, 'He's special.'

As Mimi held John gently in her arms for the first time she felt her heart flutter with a feeling of love so strong that it shocked her. Seconds later the air-raid sirens began whining and wailing. The Second World War had started in 1939 but only this month had the German airforce begun to rain bombs on London and other major British cities. Liverpool was in the firing line because it was a large seaport and a hub of industry. Nowhere in the city, not even that warm maternity ward on Oxford street, was safe from Hitler's bombs.

A chorus of startled crying babies soon joined the deafening wail of the siren. As Mimi gathered herself and said her hurried goodbyes, a nurse took John and placed him under the bed to shelter him from a possible attack.

John's early years were spent in a suburb of Liverpool called Penny Lane (later the Beatles recorded a song about the area called 'Penny Lane'). He lived in Newcastle Street in one of the hundreds of red-brick terraced houses that was home to the dock or factory workers of Liverpool. Freddy stayed away at sea for most of the war, and Julia often felt alone and struggled to raise John by herself.

The war continued to cast its grey shadow over the lives of everyone until 1945. Sometimes it felt like happiness, as well as food, clothes and petrol, was rationed because of it. Eventually, Julia found some happiness with a new boyfriend. That was when she asked Mimi to help her take care of John.

'I can't bear to let him go,' Julia sniffed into her hanky. 'But, I just can't manage by myself any longer.

*Penny Lane*

If you just had John for a little while until I find my feet... perhaps when things have settled down he'll let me have John with me.'

'Don't you worry petal,' said Mimi. 'We'll love him like he's our own. He's precious, that boy. Me and George will bring him up right.'

When John was four, his parents finally split and he went to live with his auntie Mimi and Uncle George for good.

'But mummy,' moaned John, his face all snotty and eyes full of tears. 'I want to stay here with you.'

Julia clutched John tightly in her arms. 'It'll only be for bit, my darling. You'll have fun with Uncle George and Mimi makes yummy dinners.'

'Don't care!' shouted John.

'They have a lovely house... it's dead posh. You'll have a room of your own, you lucky boy.'

'Don't want to go,' cried John.

'Sorry, sweetheart. It's just the way it has to be.' Julia grabbed John's little hand and practically yanked him down the Newcastle Road.

\*\*\*

Mimi and George lived in a more well-to-do suburb of Liverpool called Woolton. John thought it was like a different world. In Penny Lane, the front doors were always open. The noises from each household wafted out into the street – the sound of babies crying, children playing and laughing, pots or pans clattering, mixed with husbands and wives shouting at each other, cussing each other in their thick Liverpudlian. It created one almighty cacophony that could belong nowhere else but Penny Lane. In Woolton, however, it was like somebody had turned the volume down. You could actually hear the birds twitter in the tree-lined streets. The houses looked clean and sparkly and they had gardens at the front and back. Kids round here didn't have to kick cans in the street. They could escape into their own back gardens and make dens in the bushes; climb trees or play footie on the grass.

'Come here lad,' said George patting John's shoulders. John had been sobbing ever since Julia dropped him off. 'I've got a little something for you.'

John's little face instantly lit up.

'What you got Uncle George?' George grabbed his hand and took him through to the kitchen. Mimi was at the sink peeling the spuds for dinner.

'I was just getting that bag of sweets out of the pantry for John,' said Uncle George, looking a bit sheepish. It was funny. Even after all these years together Mimi had the power to scare him a little bit. Solid, dependable, no-nonsense Mimi they called her. And, by gum she lived up to her reputation. When she didn't like something she would sniff the air and her face would go all pinched. George knew the warning signs and he waited for her reaction.

True to form, Mimi's facial expression went from peaceful to pinched in a moment. 'Now then George don't get spoiling him,' she said. 'John, you can have those sweeties when you've eaten up all you dinner. And I mean ALL of it.'

John and Uncle George gave each other a knowing look. It wasn't easy getting anything past Mimi. She was the boss around here and there was no point arguing. But Mimi was as loving as she was strict. All those ticking offs and rules were just because she cared about them. And, she loved John like he was her own little boy. Later that night when John was snuggled in his eiderdown Mimi crept up to say good night.

'Come here champion,' she said gathering him in her arms for a cuddle. 'You know that Uncle George and I will always look after you.'

'Course Mimi. Love you,' whispered John.

'Love you too,' answered Mimi.

\*\*\*

John was a bright spark. And, nothing made him spark like reading books. Mimi loved books, too, so she didn't mind if he spent hours and hours with his nose between the pages of his favourite novel. John was happiest up in his room, huddled in bed reading books that were far too old for him. One of his favourites was *Alice in Wonderland*. The tale captured his imagination, and it made him think about his own dreams. Sometimes he dreamed he was flying in a plane over Liverpool looking down on everyone. In other dreams he found pots of money that he stashed in his pockets and stuffed into huge sacks that he could hardly carry. When John wasn't reading or dreaming he was drawing, writing poems or listening to the radio. All in all, life at Menlove Avenue in Woolton wasn't bad. It was when he went to school that the problems really began.

'That Lennon boy is trouble,' fumed the headmaster of Dovedale Primary school, where John went when he was five. If John wasn't leading a gang of scallywags round the playground and getting into fights, then he was at the back of the class giggling and scribbling nasty little pictures of the teachers. No matter how hard the headmaster tried, he never succeeded in pulling John into line.

'That ruffian Lennon will never amount to anything,' hissed the headmaster of Quarry Bank High, the school John went to when he was eleven. John was a frustrating pupil. He was intelligent but he just wouldn't knuckle down and work. Lessons bored him – he was happier filling notebooks with weird drawings and funny stories.

'Hopeless,' the headmaster wrote at the end of one of John's most atrocious school reports, 'Rather a clown in class... He is wasting other pupil's time.'

\*\*\*

'That's it John, I've had enough!' Mimi burst into John's bedroom, waving his latest report. She'd been up to see the headmaster – AGAIN. It was the second time that term. Mimi was fuming.

John was propped up on the bed with a book. Mimi's face had that dreaded pinched look again. Her bottom lip was trembling, too. That meant big trouble.

'Sorry Mimi,' said John. 'That headmaster gets in a real tizz about everything.'

'He says you're always give him lip. I was so ashamed. To think that you can be so cheeky to your elders! You know better than that, John.'

'He's aways giving me a hard time.'

'He says you need to buck up your ideas or he'll throw you out of school.' Mimi whole face was shaking now.

'He can chuck me out for all I care,' John was angry too now.

'I care John. You need a good education to get the best start in life...' Mimi had finally started to calm down but there was a hint of desperation in her voice. 'You MUST try harder boy.'

But no matter how often Mimi begged John to try harder at school she never managed to get him to change. Soon John had quite a reputation. Teachers grimaced when they knew John was in their class: 'That boy is all mouth!' Other parents worried that he would lead their children astray: 'Don't let our kids play with that Lennon boy – he's trouble with a capital T.' None of them realised that behind all the badness lay a whole lot of sadness.

'How you doing John?' asked Uncle George. Sweet old George could always see through John's mischief. Right now George's heart was bleeding for his nephew. John's mum had gone on holiday with that boyfriend of hers. These days Julia didn't have as much time for her son. She'd had two daughters with the boyfriend. Just that morning John had received a postcard from her. On the front there was a photograph of Blackpool tower lit up at night. Underneath was written: Greetings from Sunny Blackpool. On the back Julia had scrawled a quick message:

*Dear John,*
*Having a lovely time. The girls love playing on the beach. Wish you were here. Miss you. See you when we get back.*
*Lots of love Mum XXXX.*

'I don't understand why they didn't take me,' John said quietly. George could tell by the break in his voice that John was really hurt. 'I wouldn't be in the way. I could even help.'

George liked Julia but sometimes she was just plain thoughtless. That stupid postcard had rubbed salt into the wound. Over the years George had done his best to bring a smile to John's face. When Mimi nagged the lad he'd sneak him a few sweets. Then, on his eleventh birthday, he'd given him a bicycle. Not your second-hand tack either. It was a brand new Raleigh. Today, though, George just didn't know how to console the boy.

'Do you fancy nipping into town?' suggested George, hopefully. 'We could stop by at Woolies and pick up a book and a bag of pick 'n' mix?'

'Thanks Uncle George, that'd be fun,' John smiled thinly.

Both of them knew that sweets and books were nice but they didn't fill the emptiness in John's young life. That night in bed, John tortured himself with questions:

'Why didn't she want him? Didn't she love him enough? Did she love her daughters more?' He didn't realise that being bad, bullying other kids and acting like a thug in the playground were just ways of disguising how upset he really was.

When John was fourteen, another part of his world fell apart. Uncle George died suddenly from a brain haemorrhage. Gentle, loving George, an ally in John's constant battles with Mimi, was gone. John felt bereft.

# CHAPTER 3

Britain in the early 1950s was a different world from today. The greyness and the rationing of the war years still affected people's lives. There were no televisions and computers. Instead of CDs people listened to the radio. Young people were expected to 'put up and shut up' – which meant they had to make themselves content with very little and never complain. In those days most teenagers got themselves a hobby – something like collecting stamps, fishing, dress-making or playing a musical instrument. Other than his drawing and reading, John didn't fancy hobbies – they were for other kids, 'Let the squares collect stamps,' he'd sneer. Mimi wanted him to play the violin or piano but John didn't enjoy anything that involved taking lessons.

'Just what are you going to do with yourself, our John?' was Mimi's constant refrain.

*** 

In 1955 John was fourteen and the emptiness in his life was about to be filled with pop music. That year an American band called Bill Haley and the Comets starred in a film called *Rock Around the Clock*. The movie was about young people having wild times and fun. Rock 'n' roll music was the soundtrack to their lives. With its catchy beat and groovy guitars, this new music sounded untame. It was fresh, exciting and rebellious. No-nonsense Mimi, and many of the other hat-wearing, pinch-lipped people of her generation, thought it was shocking. John knew rock 'n' roll was where it was at. At last he'd found something that could capture him, heart and soul.

By the following year, the first king of rock 'n' roll had been crowned. With his dyed black hair, sneering top lip and gyrating hips, the American star Elvis Presley was the coolest thing in pop music. It wasn't just that he looked good; he sounded amazing too. By the time his song 'Heartbreak Hotel' went to number one in the pop charts, John was already a massive fan: 'Elvis is where it's at, man,' he'd tell his school friends. Needless to say, Mimi thought Elvis and his wiggling pelvis was a disgrace.

Soon John was copying his new hero. He put posters up on the wall of his bedroom and practised looking mean and curling his lip like Elvis in the mirror. These days he turned up at school with greased-back hair and a large quiff that flopped over his forehead. He wore tight jeans called drain-pipes and strange shoes with thick soles which made him walk with a cocky swagger.

'That Lennon boy is all mouth and tight trousers,' quipped one of the teachers at school.

'You look ridiculous,' complained Mimi, 'That bloomin' Elvis Presley has turned our lives upside down.'

'Don't you understand, Mimi?' John was scowling, 'Elvis has brought meaning to my life.'

In one way Mimi was right, though. Elvis did turn John's life upside down. Years later he admitted that if it hadn't been for Elvis he would never have picked up a guitar. At school John joined a skiffle band. Skiffle music was great because any old fool could play it. It was easy to get a band together, all you needed was a guitar, a double-bass, a wash-board (this everyday bit of household equipment stolen from your mother's laundry made a darn good sound) and a tea chest to bang like a drum. John made do borrowing other people's instruments but he longed for a guitar.

'Go on Mimi,' he'd beg, 'Get us a guitar.' But, Mimi's face would go all pinched up at the very mention of the dreaded instrument. Fortunately, John found somebody who was as enthusiastic about his new hobby as he was.

For a few years now his mother had been visiting him every week. Julia's voice was nearly as loud as her bright red hair. She had a special talent for taking fun

and laughter with her wherever she went – whether that be the grocer's shop, the hairdressers or number 251 Menlove Avenue.

'I've brought you a naughty cream cake,' Julia whispered when Mimi left the room.

'Corrr, thanks Mum,' John whispered back. 'Don't tell Mimi…' The next moment Julia screwed up her face and did her best impression of Mimi's no-nonsense scowl. She only just managed to straighten her face before Mimi returned.

'What are you two giggling at?' Mimi looked puzzled.

'Nothing…' spluttered the naughty pair.

'I don't know, I swear you two are as thick as thieves. If I didn't know better I'd think Julia was your big sister, John – your naughty big sister at that!'

\*\*\*

As time passed John's love for his mother grew stronger. Not only did they lark about together; they shared a passion for music.

'My mum digs Elvis,' John boasted to his friends, whose own mothers thought Elvis was a freak of nature. Julia liked 'the king' so much she'd even named her new kitten after him. John was chuffed to bits to have such a cool mum.

'How's it going with that band of yours, our John?' asked Julia. They were sitting in the living room at Auntie Mimi's.

'Cool, mum,' John's face lit up. 'I reckon if you show me a few more of those chords on the banjo then I'll blow the other guys in the band away.'

'Right sit yourself down and contentrate, John,' Julia did her best to be firm. Her young firebrand of a son was hard work to tame. John smirked.

'I mean it, if you want to play well then you've got to watch carefully and you must practise.'

With that Julia got out her beaten up old banjo and patiently showed John a few more chords.

'You try now,' she coaxed and John picked up the banjo, stumbling to find the frets his mother had shown him.

'Blimey,' laughed Julia, 'You strum that poor thing like you're itching a rash. Treat it gently.'

John tried again, but he was so rough one of the strings went TWANG.

'Another string's broken, John.' Julia tried to brush aside her impatience. 'Honestly, the sooner you get your own guitar the better. My poor banjo just isn't up to the job.'

Eventually, John scraped enough money together to buy himself a guitar.

'My mum bought it for me,' he lied to Mimi – it was the only way to keep her off his back about the matter.

The guitar was one of those cheap ones that could be bought by mail order, but to John it was everything – he was ready to rock. At school, he formed a new skiffle band called the Black Jacks. Later, they changed their name to the Quarry Men and began to get a few live gigs at church halls and youth clubs. Even when John began to rake in a few shillings for playing, Mimi remained stern and disapproving.

'The guitar is alright for a hobby John,' Mimi moaned. 'But you'll never make a living from it.'

'Mimi, I don't care about the future,' he shouted back. 'I'm having a good time. Why can't you just stop nagging and let me enjoy myself?'

And John was enjoying himself. For the first time, his pockets were jangling with money. And, best of all, being in a band meant you got noticed by the girls – and John was a real one for the girls, especially blondes who looked like his favourite pin-up, the French movie actress, Brigitte Bardot.

Rock 'n' roll gradually took over John's life. The little interest that he'd had in his school work disappeared as soon as he picked up the guitar. It came as no surprise to Mimi when John failed every single one of his nine O-level exams.

'Oh John,' she wailed, 'What are you going to do? You need a proper job.'

'I'm going to be a pop star, Mimi,' he told her, winning her over with one of his best boyish grins.

# CHAPTER 4

Saturday 6th July 1957 was a beautiful sunny day. The warm weather had drawn a large crowd to the garden fête at St Peter's Parish Church in Woolton. A small raised stage had been set up between the stalls and a whole day of entertainment was promised. The highlight was the fancy dress parade and the crowning of the Rose Queen. After that a local brass band were going to play. Then, there was a display by Liverpool police dogs. Later still, the Quarry Men were going to treat Woolton to some of their best foot-stomping tunes. John was really excited because he was going to play one of his favourite songs live for the first time. It was called 'Be Bop a Lula' and it was really rockin'.

In the audience that day was a dark-haired lad called

Paul McCartney. He was a bit younger than John – and certainly not as cool – but he could play the the guitar, trumpet and piano. He knew far more chords on the guitar than John did, too. When the Quarry Men stopped for an interval, Paul's friend introduced him to John. Before long the two young men had struck up an excited conversation about music.

'I could teach you some proper chords,' Paul told John. It was a brave thing to say but even John had to admit that all he could play was the chords he'd learned on the banjo.

'Show us what you can do then,' John dared the younger man.

Paul grabbed the guitar and began playing 'Twenty Flight Rock'. As his fingers raced across the fret board there was a stunned silence. Paul's playing blew John's version of 'Be Bop a Lula' away. John went slightly pale and had to admit to himself that this young bloke could play better than him. He didn't look half bad either – a bit like Elvis.

John was used to being the leader of the Quarry Men. He also liked to think of himself as the best musician in the band. Meeting Paul had unsettled him. That night as John lay in bed, he wondered what his next move should be. Should he invite McCartney to join his band? John felt slightly threatened by the younger man's talent. Yet, deep down inside, he knew that Paul would be good for the band.

'Who knows?' he mused, 'With Paul at my side we could become the best band ever.' As John drifted off to sleep, his head was filled with dreams of being a popstar. The next morning he decided he would give the kid a chance after all.

Over the next few months, John and Paul met up regularly and played music together. Most days, they were huddled round a small record-player with American tunes blaring; or teaching each other what they knew on the guitar. They often practised in Paul's front room. Paul's mother had died when he was a young boy so the house was empty during the day. Paul's father worried about his son's relationship with John. His lad was a bit of a brainbox and doing well at school. If he kept it up, then, who knows, he'd make university – his mother Mary would have been so proud. The only spanner in the works was that troublemaker, John Lennon. Paul's work had gone downhill since that young blade had been on the scene.

Meanwhile, back at Menlove Avenue, the subject up

for discussion each and every day was John's crummy school reports and his failed exams. Fortunately, the new headmaster of Quarry Bank thought there was a glimmer of hope for the young rebel. He suggested John should go to art college. By now John wasn't too fussed about drawing and painting either, but going to college was a cunning way of avoiding getting a job – the girls were supposed to be good-looking too!

So at sixteen, John said goodbye to Quarry Bank High and enrolled at Liverpool School of Art. From his first day at college John made no effort to fit in or conform to the rules. He lolloped into classes when he felt like it and messed about.

'What are you going to do with your life, Lennon?' barked the metalwork teacher one day.

'I'm going to be a pop star, sir,' John sneered, as the teacher raised his eyes to the ceiling.

At college, John made some new friends. One person that John particularly looked up to was Stuart Sutcliffe. He was a quiet, good-looking bloke with a tremendous creative streak. The college tutors thought he had a bright future ahead of him as a painter or a sculptor. Many people thought John and Stuart were unlikely best mates. John was loud and threatening, while Stuart was gentle and sensitive. Yet the two men hit it off because, deep down inside, John was as caring and thoughtful as his new friend.

When John wasn't hanging out at coffee bars and local pubs with Stuart, then he was playing with the Quarry Men. Paul McCartney proved a hit with the band but they needed another guitarist. It was Paul that introduced George Harrison to the group.

'Blimey,' wailed John when he met George for the first time. 'He looks about eight. I bet he doesn't even shave yet.'

'I'm fourteen, mate,' George replied, trying to sound more confident than actually he felt. This John Lennon bloke was a bit scary.

'Fancy yourself as a popstar then George?' John said in a slightly superior way. Since John had started at art college he believed he was a man, a real grown-up – not a boy, like the awkward little lad in front of him.

'Yeah,' said George feebly.

'Go on then, show us what you can do,' said John with a hint of impatience.

George grabbed his guitar. There wasn't a moment to lose. He wanted to prove to this brash friend of Paul's that he had what it took – and more.

As soon as he began playing, it was obvious that George had incredible talent. John could only stand back and admire the sounds that the young bloke created as his slim fingers picked and strummed at the strings of the guitar.

'Wow,' said John, as George finished playing. 'You certainly know how to make that thing sing. You're in the band.'

'Hey, thanks,' George looked thrilled. 'That's great!'

'Yeah,' added John, 'But try to look older than your shoe size. We're a proper band, not a boy band.'

Soon Paul and George were bunking off school to practise with John. Sometimes they played in the college coffee bar. Other times they crammed into George or Paul's house and began writing songs together. None of them knew where their music was taking them but they were having such a good time they didn't stop to think about the future.

Then, in July 1958, something terrible happened and the future crashed for John. It was just an ordinary day when Julia nipped over to Menlove Avenue for a chat and catch up with Mimi. After a quick gossip she was on her way. She'd been smiling and waving at the front gate one minute then the next there was a dreadful sound of locked brakes, then tyres skidding, followed by an ominous thud.

'I couldn't stop,' whimpered the driver, an off-duty policeman on his way home after work.

'I heard the screech of the brakes,' cried Mimi, who'd rushed through the gate to find Julia in a huddle on the floor near the bus stop. There was blood everywhere.

'I think she's dead,' said a passerby who bent down to check Julia's pulse. By now her face was drained of life. Yet somehow, her red hair seemed even more vibrant than usual.

The only person who couldn't speak was John. He didn't say anything. For once, he was so numb with shock that he was lost for words. The mother he had lost as a boy was now lost to him for ever.

Paul McCartney knew what it was like to lose your mother. Now the two young men were bonded by pain as well as music. From this time onwards their friendship became even closer. They both tried their best to shrug off the hurt they felt inside. Yet, the ache was never far away.

Not long after the death of his mother John met another person who could see his gentler side. John first saw Cynthia Powell in lettering class at college.

'Cyn's a real square and a little bit posh,' John admitted to Stuart.

Though she was quiet and studious, he was still attracted by her good looks.

As for John, he might seem wild and arrogant, but she liked him too: 'John's a bit rough and pretends he's working-class,' Cynthia confided in her best friend.

'I could fall in love with you,' John told Cynthia on one of their first dates. They were sitting in one of the new trendy milkbars in Liverpool. You could hang out in these places all afternoon, drinking coffees and listening to rock 'n' roll on the jukebox. These days John and Cynthia spent precious hours staring into each other's eyes.

'Funny that,' said Cynthia, her eyes wide and starry. 'I could fall for you too, John Lennon.'

'Is that why you dyed your hair blonde?' John reached over the table and took a lock of her hair in his fingers. Cynthia giggled girlishly.

'Well, I know you like Brigitte Bardot.'

'Now you're talking,' laughed John.

John and Cynthia whiled away many hours in coffee bars. Though they seemed poles apart, they found they had many things in common.

'I find it hard to talk about my father dying,' Cynthia told John one rainy afternoon.

'I can't talk about Julia to anyone,' John admitted.

'You can tell me anything John,' Cynthia tried to coax the words out of him.

'I know,' said John, but still he didn't open up. Perhaps if he did, too much hurt and pain would come out. It was better to live life as if all that mattered was having fun. And right now, with this gorgeous girl and his guitar at his side, he felt that the good times were about to roll.

# CHAPTER 5

In 1959 many of the clubs in Liverpool were for jazz bands. 'Those places are just for old bores,' moaned John. 'What this city needs is a place where we can play pop music!'

John's prayers were answered when The Casbah Club opened.

'It's really just a coffee bar in a basement,' said Paul excitedly, 'but they're looking for live acts'.

'Great!' John was really enthusiastic. 'We could make this place our place if we wanted.'

And they did. John, Paul and George helped to decorate the dingy basement before the big opening night. Each wall was stripped and painted a different bright colour. On the big night the three young men played together in front of a live audience for the first time. They didn't have a drummer, so they asked the son of the owner of the Casbah, Pete Best, to help out. He was good-looking. The band looked great together. Things looked set to go well.

The Quarry Men went down a storm and they were signed up to play the Casbah for a few months. Very soon they had fans coming back to see them again and again. Most of the girls thought Paul was really cute but they had mixed feelings about John – he made them laugh but he was a bit scary. Dressed in black with dark sunglasses, he looked like a real cool dude; he was also the joker in the band – he had a cracking sense of humour. Together, the two frontmen were a force to be reckoned with. They belted out their songs and the crowd always cheered for more.

Behind the scenes there were all kinds of shuffles and changes taking place. Even though John's art-school friend Stuart couldn't play a note of music, John wanted him in the band to play bass guitar.

'Don't worry,' John said, 'I'll teach you the chords.'

Stuart did worry but he still joined the band. To hide the fact that he couldn't really play he performed with his back to the audience. Now that the band was getting popular they also needed a catchy name.

'The Quarry Men was alright for a group of school boys but we're going to be bigger than that,' John said, and what John said actually went.

For a few gigs they called themselves 'Johnny and the Moondogs' but it didn't sound right either.

'"Buddy Holly and the Crickets" is a cool name,' John told the others. 'We should think of something like that.' Soon afterwards, John and Stuart came up with 'The Beatals' – a play on the word 'beetle' because they were a 'beat' band. This soon changed again, to the 'Silver Beetles'. Then, one day, John suggested that they should just be 'The Beatles'.

'It's simple, it's cool,' John persuaded the others, 'A name people will remember.' Little did he know how important the name would become in the history of pop music.

After their stint at the Casbah, the Beatles went on tour for the first time. Squashed into an old van, the band travelled to Scotland to play at a long list of damp dance halls, pokey pubs and cold church halls. It wasn't glamorous and they often played to a handful of people, but the Beatles were having fun. They had holes in their shoes and their clothes had seen better days yet they felt like they were about to make it.

'We ain't made it quite yet, boyo,' John told George when they returned to Liverpool. For a few months they struggled to get gigs, until one day they were asked to play in the German city of Hamburg – for ordinary lads from Liverpool, it seemed like an invitation to the big time.

To start with, 'the big time' meant playing eight-hour sessions at a club called the Indra. The tiny club was in a seedy part of Hamburg which only came alive at night. It was a place where the men got into fights and the women wore too much make-up and not enough clothes. Auntie Mimi's face would have pinched up at the very thought of her nephew being let loose in such a wicked place.

Mimi would not have approved of John's new lifestyle either. These days he stayed up all night drinking too much beer. After the long hours playing at the Indra he crawled back with the rest of the band to sleep in a run-down dirty old cinema. They made do by washing in the sinks of the ladies toilets.

\*\*\*

'One, two, one, two, three, four,' John shouted into the microphone as the Beatles began a fast rock 'n' roll number. His voice sounded hoarse from singing all night long but the crowd loved the raw energy of the band. The Beatles were now playing another club in Hamburg called the Kaiserkeller. Some days they hit the stage at two o'clock in the afternoon and didn't leave until the early hours the next morning. John found it exhausting but it was exhilarating because they were attracting bigger crowds. Best of all, they were learning new tricks all the time.

Amongst their fans was a group of artists and students. Astrid Kirchherr was a photographer. She had short cropped blonde hair and cool black leather clothes. John thought she was gorgeous. Eventually Astrid became Stuart's girlfriend but she was a good friend to all the band. She showed them around Hamburg and regularly took their photographs. These days the boys sported leather jackets and trousers and black cowboy boots. Astrid's pictures captured their mean and moody look. They also showed a hunger in John's eyes – a deep and desperate longing for success.

The Beatles grew up in Hamburg. After a few months, though, it all came to a sudden end. The

German authorities discovered that George was too young to work and they sent him packing, back to England. Then they discovered that none of the band had work permits so they had to leave town, too.

'It's no good moping my boy,' Mimi told John. He'd been back from Hamburg a few weeks. Ever since his return he'd been sulking – the air in Menlove Avenue was thick with tension. Not even Cynthia could bring John out of his black mood.

'You need to find a JOB!' nagged Mimi.

'Don't you get it Mimi?' John shouted, 'Music *is* my job!'

'Well, if that's the case,' suggested Mimi, 'why not get in touch with the other boys?'

'I know,' said John. 'I'm still trying to decide if the Beatles have a future or not.'

'There's only one way to find out…' and with that Mimi left John to his stormy thoughts.

# CHAPTER 6

In 1961 a tiny sweaty club in Liverpool called the Cavern was where it was at. Even though it stank of disinfectant and toilets and lots of people hit their heads on the low ceilings, the Cavern was attracting packs of excited teenagers. Word had got out that an amazing new band was playing there regularly. People were saying that the Beatles were going to be the next big thing in pop music. OK, the band looked a bit strange. They needed haircuts and their clothes had obviously never seen an iron. But, when they played, they sounded fantastic.

People said that the screech of their guitars could send tingles down your spine. They said that John and Paul's wild singing was electrifying. But most of all, they said that the frantic beat made you want to move your feet like never before.

When people came to see the Beatles play at the Cavern they weren't disappointed. They came back for more, and brought their friends. Very soon, Beatles fans were queuing up around the block just to get into the smelly little club. They dashed there in their lunchtime to catch the band's daily session. Then they come back in the evening to listen to the Beatles play again.

'They say we're Liverpool's favourite band,' Paul told the others excitedly.

'Hey,' John replied. 'We might be famous after all.'

It was during one of these lunchtime sessions that Auntie Mimi finally came to see what her wilful nephew was up to. As she entered the tiny basement room she had to stoop in case she ruined her hat.

'Watch yourself old gal,' said one cheeky young man. Mimi gave him one of her most no-nonsense stares and looked down to make sure her cardigan was neatly buttoned up.

Mimi was out of place amongst the girls with their short skirts with lashings of eyeliner and mascara. And, she certainly didn't expect to catch any admiring glances from any of the men in here. Hmmph, they looked such a mess in their scruffy shirts and tight trousers.

'Mind you, look at the state of John,' she muttered to herself. 'He isn't any better.'

Mimi stood back in the shadows as her boy and the rest of the band walked onto the tiny stage. As usual, John was in his crumpled up black polo-neck and jeans. He didn't look up to much and Mimi expected even less of his performance.

'I'm nothing if not fair,' thought Mimi as John began

to play the guitar. 'This rock 'n' roll music isn't my thing, but let's see what the boy can do.'

Mimi watched as John's peformance lit up the stage. And, as she stood there she felt the same stirrings of love and pride that she felt all those years ago when she had first seen him as a baby. There was something special about John. Eyes followed him everywhere, drinking in his performance.

'John,' she said when she went back stage to see him afterwards. 'I think you did very well.'

'Thanks Auntie,' said John, as he gave her a little hug. That was praise indeed, coming from Mimi. 'Does that mean you approve of my job now?'

'I didn't say that,' Mimi added, defensively. 'I still reckon that music is OK for a hobby but not as a real career.'

'I'll show you Mimi.'

'Mmmm, we'll see.' And she stomped off before he could get another word in.

That April the Beatles returned to Hamburg for a few months. Once again, they were playing seedy clubs and staying up all night. By the end of the trip, Stuart and Astrid had fallen madly in love.

'This time tomorrow we'll back in lovely Liverpool,'

John told Stu after their final gig. Stu looked slightly uneasy.

'John,' he began sheepishly. 'I'm not going back to England.'

'Come off it,' said John, 'You're not staying here are you?'

'I want to be with Astrid. She means the world to me. Who knows, I might make it as an artist, too.'

'But what about the band Stu?' John's face was pale.

'Astrid comes first now. I don't have the same drive and ambition as you. Music is in your blood, John. I'm sure the Beatles will make it. But I'm just not cut out for rock 'n' roll.'

'I'm sure going to miss you Stu – but you were never that good anyway, eh?' John forced a laugh, as he tried to make light of how upset he felt that his best mate was quitting the band.

\*\*\*

Back in Liverpool the buzz about the Beatles was felt everywhere. People wanted to know all about them. John wrote a funny article about the band for a local magazine called *Mersey Beat*: 'Once upon a time there were three little boys called John, George and Paul,' he wrote. 'They decided to get together because they were the getting together type. When they were together they wondered what for, after all, what for? So all of a sudden they all grew guitars and formed a noise.'

In October that year 'the noise' was heard for the first time by Brian Epstein, the son of one of Liverpool's most well-off store owners. Compared to the Beatles, Brian was posh, or even 'upper class'. He was the kind of bloke that John would have teased at school. But Brian had been to private school, and these days he ran the family music shop, North End Music Stores. He liked classical music but he always tried to keep an eye on what was happening in the pop scene. He prided himself on having the best selection of records on sale in the north of England.

He'd noticed that a few people had come into the shop and asked for records by the Beatles. 'Odd name for a band,' he thought dismisively. Even so, he decided he should check them out. One of the girls serving in the shop laughed out loud. 'Don't you remember them Mr Epstein?' she grinned, 'You used to kick them out the shop for hanging around and making too much noise.'

'The Beatles?,' said one of his friends. 'They're the

greatest. They're at the Cavern this week...'

When Brian saw the Beatles play at the Cavern he was baffled: 'What scruff bags,' was his first impression. 'Awfully coarse and rough,' was his next impression. And, to cap it all, 'They can't play!'

All in all, Brian was mystified by the fuss surrounding the Beatles. Yet, over the following weeks he found himself being drawn back to the smoky club again and again to hear them play. Gradually, he became fascinated by them, especially John.

Backstage, in the dressing-room the band couldn't help wondering what Brian was up to.

'What's that toff doing here again?' George asked.

'Dunno,' replied John, 'Maybe he wants to be our manager or something.'

'That would be great,' enthused Paul. After all, they didn't really have a manager.

'As long as he doesn't expect us to wear posh suits like him,' muttered John, with a scowl on his face.

In December 1961, Brian Epstein became the Beatles' manager. Suddenly, the four scruffs were being told to smarten up their act. They had haircuts and Brian got them to wear proper trousers rather than their smelly old jeans or worn-out leathers.

'No more eating, swearing or smoking on stage,' Brian insisted. 'And, when you've finished the set you bow to the audience.'

John nearly choked on his cheese sandwich when he heard that, but Brian pointed out that unless they polished themselves up then they wouldn't be able to play bigger and smarter venues. And, until they were seen in better places, he wouldn't be able to find them a proper record deal. John's heart was set on a record deal, so for the first time in his life he 'shut up and put up' and did what he was told.

By the beginning of 1962, things were looking up. Brian was often down in London talking with the big chiefs at record companies or music newspapers. If anybody could get them a record deal or publicity, then it seemed Brian could. While Brian worked on the Beatles' future, the band began writing more of their own songs. When they played live, they usually covered old rock 'n' roll numbers written by other musicians. This was normal in those days but John and Paul thought it would be interesting to try doing their own thing. Sometimes when they were practising together beautiful tunes would seem to appear out of nowhere. If one of them thought of an interesting melody then the other could add to it and create something more special.

Writing songs together brought John and Paul even closer. This new bond with Paul meant that John didn't miss his old mate Stuart as much. At least until April 1962 when there was terrible news from Hamburg: Stuart Sutcliffe had died after suffering a massive brain haemorrhage. It had been quick and final. All the Beatles were stunned but it was worse for John – Stuart had been his dearest friend. Once again, he had lost somebody close to him. The shock was terrible; but, after years of hiding his emotions, he knew how to disguise the pain.

Three days after Stuart's death, the Beatles were back playing live in Hamburg. This time they were at the Star Club and they were performing alongside big name acts like Gene Vincent and Little Richard. As usual, John put his heart and soul into the music and played the comedian between songs. Only those who really knew him could guess how hard it was for him to perform.

# CHAPTER 7

The year 1962 was a roller-coaster ride for John. It started on a high with the promise of record deals and success. Whenever anyone in the band got down and questioned what was going to happen next, John had a good way of cheering them all up:

'Where are we going fellas?' he'd ask.

'To the top, Johnny!' the rest of the band would shout.

'Where's that, fellas?'

'To the toppermost of the poppermost!' they yelled back.

'Right, let's go!' John shouted and everyone fell about laughing.

After Stuart's death, life had seemed to hurtle downwards but just before it hit rock bottom the most exciting and thrilling news came through. The boys were still in Hamburg when Brian sent them a telegram telling them that he'd secured a contract to record for EMI records on the Parlaphone label: 'EMI CONTRACT SIGNED, SEALED. TREMENDOUS IMPORTANCE TO US ALL. WONDERFUL.' Suddenly, the skies were the limit. John wrote a brief postcard back to Brian: 'When are we going to be millionaires?'

That June the Beatles auditioned for a producer at Parlaphone. His name was George Martin. Like Brian, he had a posh accent and preferred classical music. From the early days the Beatles jokingly called him 'The Duke of Edinburgh'. But, if the boys had any doubts about what the man who looked and sounded like a private school teacher could do for their music, then they kept quiet and allowed George to guide them.

'I don't see why the Duke wants us to dump Pete,' moaned John when George asked the band to get rid of Pete Best.

'Pete isn't the best drummer in the world,' Paul tried to reason. 'Ringo Starr on the other hand would be great.'

'What, that short bloke with Rory Storm and the

Hurricanes? Bit old, isn't he?'

'Nah,' said Paul. 'He's all right. Not bad on the drums. Can even sing a bit. And he's got a sense of humour.'

'Mmm,' John looked thoughtful. 'Well, if the big wigs think we need a new drummer we better do as they say. Can't risk losing the contract.'

\*\*\*

With Ringo Starr on board, the Beatles were complete. Meanwhile, John had problems closer to home. Cynthia had been his girlfriend since art school. Commitment to the band and long trips to Hamburg meant that they'd often been apart. In truth, John wasn't always faithful to Cynthia when he was away but they were in love enough to stay together. That August Cynthia had some serious news for John.

'We weren't careful enough,' she said, her eyes welling with tears. 'I'm pregnant.' In those days young people were expected to get married if a girl 'got in the family way'. Even young men with aspirations to be the 'top-permost of the poppermost' had to face up to their responsibilities and do the right thing – which was to get married. 'Don't worry, Cyn,' John reassured her, 'I'll make an honest woman of ya.' Even as he said it, he wondered what he was going to tell Mimi.

Later that day Mimi, the Queen of no-nonsense, exploded with rage. But, when she finally calmed down, she offered to buy a wedding ring for Cynthia and suggested that she move into Menlove Avenue.

That same month John and Cynthia got married in a registry office in Liverpool. Throughout the service the young couple giggled uncontrollably. For John it was nerve-racking taking on this responsibility when so much else was going on in his life. After lunch at a local restaurant, John took off with the rest of the band for a gig in Chester. Dashing off to be a Beatle set the pattern for the rest of their marriage. By now John was twenty-one years old. He had never planned on being a husband so young. He'd always dreamed of getting rich or being a famous pop star. Fame and marriage didn't really go hand in hand. Brian suggested that they keep the wedding a secret so that female Beatles fans wouldn't be upset. John went along with the ruse and Cynthia remained in the background while he was on the road or making records in London.

As the summer of 1962 drew to an end, the Beatles

were in a hot and sticky Abbey Road Studio 3 in London, recording the song that would be their first hit record. John and Paul had written 'Love Me Do' when they were just teenagers bunking off school. Now they were older, the song sounded a bit raw and simple. While they recorded the song they all felt very nervous. John reckoned you could hear him qu-qu-quaking in his boots as he played the harmonica. Paul thought you could hear the tr-tr-trembling in his voice.

George Martin wasn't convinced that 'Love Me Do' was hit material but when it was released that October it went straight into the UK singles chart at number 49. By Christmas it reached its top position of number seventeen in the charts. At the time John felt like he'd reached the top of the roller-coaster – he didn't realise this was just the beginning of the climb to the top.

Over the next months the Beatles found themselves whipped up and stirred into a frenzy of action. Television appearances where followed by hours in the studio at Abbey Road recording new songs for their first album. They whizzed back to Hamburg for more live shows and set off on another tour of Scotland. They snatched precious moments on the tour bus or in their hotel rooms to write new material. The magic ingredient in all their songs was keeping things simple. 'We need to get words like "me" and "you" in each number,' John reckoned. In March 1963 another one of their self-penned records 'Please Please Me' went to number one in the UK singles charts. Even the music press loved them. Headlines ran: 'Liverpool's Finest!', 'The Fab Four!', 'The Beatles are Coming!'. Soon afterwards the Beatles made the front cover of the supercool music paper *The Record Mirror*.

'We polish up nicely for four lads from Liverpool,' said Paul as he gawped at the cover photo.

'Fame at last,' John sighed.

That spring Cynthia gave birth to a baby boy, called Julian. 'Oh, Mimi.' Cynthia was cuddling her tiny newborn son. 'I wish John was here to see him.'

'Hmmph, off with that bloomin' band again,' muttered Mimi. 'No matter, little one, your daddy will be home soon.'

It took three days for John to finally meet his son. 'My beautiful boy,' said John as he held Julian close to his chest for the first time. 'I'm going to be the best dad.'

'I know you will,' Cynthia beamed.

'If you're around,' added Mimi, who couldn't resist a little dig.

Sadly, John *wasn't* around to be the best dad. Inevitably, being a Beatle took over any family life that he did have. 'Sorry Cyn,' he'd say, as he was leaving her at home with Julian and Mimi for what seemed like the millionth time, 'But fame has its price.' He always said it with a big grin on his face so everyone believed he was having the time of his life.

# CHAPTER 8

The rest of 1963 was extraordinary for John and the Beatles. In September, 'She Loves You' went straight to the top of the singles charts. Then the LP 'Please Please Me' went to number one in the album charts. The Beatles had become so famous that they were invited to perform in front of the royal family at the Royal Variety Performance. 'Can you believe it?' croaked Paul, 'Little old us playing in front of the Queen Mum and Princess Margaret?'

As it happened, nobody could believe it by the end of their performance. By now the Beatles looked respectable in their neat suits. The crowd were delighted when they sang their number one hit. They laughed heartily when Paul entertained them with his

Liverpudlian humour. The Beatles even managed to charm them with their bows at the end of the act. But John shocked everybody when he made a gibe at the royal family – in those days that simply wasn't the done thing.

'The ones in the cheap seats, clap their hands,' John told the people in the audience as he introduced one of their songs.

'The rest of you just rattle yer jewellery,' he added, as he looked up at the royal box.

The next day John's naughty dig at the royal family made front-page news. 'What a cheek,' some people thought. 'Oh, well, it's just harmless fun,' said his fans; but already John had been singled out as the Beatle with the big mouth.

By Christmas the Beatles were back at number one in the single charts with 'I Want to Hold Your Hand'. In a matter of months, John and the boys had become hot property. Everywhere they went, hoards of teenagers massed to see them. Sometimes there were even riots and the Beatles had to peg it as fast as they could before the fans got to them. Suddenly, packs of charging teenagers were as dangerous and life-threatening as swarms of killer bees.

At Beatles concerts, row upon row of screaming girls cried out for their favourite Beatle. 'I love you John!' they yelled; or 'Paul, yeh, yeh, yeh!' Sometimes young women were so overcome with excitement that they fainted and had to be pulled from the crowd. Nurses had to be stationed at the end of each row at concerts to deal with the poor overcome creatures. By the end of the year, the screams and cheers at the concerts were so deafening that the band could hardly hear what they were playing.

'It wouldn't matter if I never sang,' moaned John. 'Often I don't anyway. I just stand there and move my mouth. I reckon we could send out four wax-work dummies of ourselves and nobody would notice.' In a way, he was right, the fans didn't seem to care – they were just there to scream and stare. Nobody had ever seen scenes like these in Britain before. One journalist called the new phenomenon 'Beatlemania'.

The Beatles exploded into the hearts and souls of millions of teenagers. Not everybody liked what they heard and saw of the cheeky young men from Liverpool, though. Some parents feared that listening to the Beatles was a bad influence on their children. The Beatles certainly looked smarter than they did in their Cavern days but many older people thought it was mad the way teenagers copied the band's style or wasted their money on band paraphernalia. These days young men came home from the barber's shop sporting the Beatles hairstyle, or 'mop-top', as it became known. One head-master at a grammar school made it a school rule that anyone with a Beatles haircut would be sent home immediately. Unfortunately, all this disapproval only seemed to make the Beatles more popular with their fans. 'We feel as if the Beatles belong to us rather than our parents,' young people explained.

The crazy exhilarating sensation called Beatlemania spread throughout Europe and by the beginning of 1964 it had swept to the USA. In the 1950s American teenagers had screamed their hearts out for the King of Rock 'n' Roll, Elvis Presley. Now, they had four young princes of pop to idolize and people were saying that the Beatles were even bigger than Elvis. It all began with the release of 'I Want To Hold Your Hand', which went to number one in the American singles chart in February 1964. A week later, the Beatles boarded a plane to the USA to begin their first American tour.

Nobody, let alone the Beatles, was prepared for the welcome they would receive from American fans. As the fab four stepped down from the plane at New York's

Kennedy Airport their eyes nearly popped with wonder.

'Wow,' said John. 'There must be thousands of them out there.' On the plane over they had been told there was a big crowd waiting for them, but this exceeded any of their dreams.

'Blimey,' muttered Paul, who felt excited and nervous all at the same time. 'I can't believe it. They can't all be here for *us*.'

'*We* were told an English band couldn't make it in America,' John continued. 'But, come on, this has got to prove them wrong. If we can crack America then we can conquer the world!!'

At the airport that day there were about 5,000 fans waiting to catch a glimpse of their favourite band; and in the next few weeks fans followed the Beatles everywhere they went. When they appeared on a top American TV show the streets surrounding the television studio were swamped with so many excited teenagers that they brought the traffic to a halt.

At one hotel where they stayed, 10,000 fans gathered outside in the hope of catching a fleeting glance of their favourite Beatle.

'These Yanks are wild,' said John, in the back of the limo as they left the hotel. By now the fans were flinging themselves at the car like moths at a light at night.

'Apparently, it's our hair that sends them so wild,' Ringo joked.

'It's like being in a film.' John looked disbelieving. 'It doesn't feel like it's really happening to us.'

In Britain the Beatles had only ever played in front of 2,000 people. Now they were performing in front of 20,000 people. The band could hardly hear a note for the cries of 'We want the Beatles!'

'We want the Beatles, we want the Beatles!' mimicked John in the dressing–room, after playing one of their

American gigs. He didn't look very happy. Fans back at home had pelted them with jelly babies when they'd heard that these were their favourite sweets. At this concert the fans had bombarded them with jelly beans. 'They felt more like rounds of bullets being fired at us than sweets,' complained John who was covered in tiny bruises. 'I know I wanted to be famous but that was ridiculous.'

For the first time, John was having doubts about how big the Beatles were becoming. Now that they were 'the toppermost of the poppermost', they spent most of their time running away from fans or skulking in hotel rooms. Worse of all, they were made to attend posh dos with the kind of people that John hated.

'I didn't start a band so that I could mix with snooty types,' he moaned. Sometimes, when he felt this low John yearned for the days when they had played live in Hamburg or at the Cavern. 'We were just four young lads having a laugh, playing rock 'n' roll.'

Now, fame seemed to be sucking the fun out of everything and John was becoming desperate.

# CHAPTER 9

Although John questioned fame and the direction that his career was taking, he did enjoy the money that his success brought him. By the middle of 1964, number one records at home and abroad meant that he was already a millionaire. To escape the prying eyes of the fans he bought a mansion-style home for his family in Surrey. It had a swimming pool and large gardens where he could be private and quiet.

John didn't carry money around with him but he did enjoy dropping in on shops and telling them to bill him later. Amongst his favourite shopping sprees were those for books to fill the lengths of empty shelves in his new home. He also loved buying new guitars, unusual musical instruments, recording equipment and televisions –

Cynthia thought he was mad, but John insisted upon a television in every room of the house. For all his new wealth, though, John still fell back on some of his old ways. He preferred yummy fry-ups to fancy food and he asked Mimi to buy his hair combs from the market in Penny Lane in Liverpool because 'they're the best'.

One of John's biggest extravagances were his cars. 'The Mini is for pottering around in,' he told a journalist, 'the Rolls for relaxing in, and the Ferrari for zoom.' John didn't drive much himself but he loved lolling in the back of his psychedelic (a word for a mish-mash of garish colours whipped up into a swirly whirly pattern guaranteed to make your eyes go zing) chauffeur-driven Rolls, using his feet to make the electric window go up and down. One day he was in the car when a group of fans began smearing the outside with lipstick graffiti. Soon, the excited mob were bumping and jostling one another and denting the bodywork.

'Blimey,' complained the driver, 'I'm going to put a stop to that lot.'

'No, leave them alone,' John said calmly. 'They bought the car. They've got a right to smash it up.'

Another day John's psychedelic Rolls Royce pulled up outside Mimi's house on Menlove Avenue in Liverpool.

'Get in, Auntie, I'm going to buy you a new house,' John said proudly. Of late, Beatles fans had been surrounding John's old home and pestering Mimi on the telephone. John had promised his auntie he'd buy her a place away from it all. Mimi wanted to live by the sea in Poole in the south of England. True to his word, John bought Mimi a lovely little cottage on the coast.

'You never thought you'd see the day,' he told Mimi, as he handed her the keys to her new home.

'You're right there, John,' answered Mimi, 'But, is all this success making you happy? You're hardly ever at home. You're like a stranger to your own son – you don't even know how old he is.'

'I'm tough enough to take it,' John told her, but Mimi knew that deep inside John was gentle and sensitive. Just as she had worried about his future when he was a boy, Mimi fretted about what lay ahead for John now that he was a man.

# CHAPTER 10

'Paul writes the tear-jerkers,' John told the journalist, 'and I write the gritty stuff.' In yet another interview with the press, John was the Beatle who was doing the talking. He always had something intelligent to say and if you got him on a good day then he just kept on going – it usually made an interesting story. What most people wanted to know was how John and Paul had become the most successful writing duo ever.

'It's not brain surgery,' John told the journalist. 'We're just ripping off other writers.'

In fact, although all Beatles songs were credited to 'Lennon/McCartney', John and Paul rarely wrote a whole song together. They helped each other but they had such different styles that they usually composed alone. Paul liked love songs or ballads that made you go all gooey inside. He wrote slow numbers like 'Yesterday' and 'Eleanor Rigby'.

John was always reading. Even if he was slumped in the back of a tour bus or waiting to go on stage he usually had his nose in a newspaper or book. Inspired by the things he read, his lyrics were often more difficult to understand than Paul's. The words of 'Lucy in the Sky With Diamonds', for example were influenced by one of John's favourite children's books, 'Through the Looking Glass'. In 'Day in a Life' his strange lyrics were inspired by stories he'd read in the newspaper.

John became famous for the songs that made you think but he also wrote about his own life. In 'Strawberry Fields' and 'In My Life', he took a trip back to his childhood and wrote about the places he had hung out in when he was a boy.

Many people assumed that because John didn't write the same kind of soppy songs as Paul that he was harder. Even when he sang about his insecurities, people did not hear his sadness. In the song 'Help', John talked about losing grip of his life and needing support from his friends. Many people just thought he'd written another good pop song. In 'Nowhere Man', he showed his increasing unhappiness by singing about living in a nowhere land, with nowhere plans for nobody. But most people believed that John was being John and writing quirky lyrics again.

As the 1960s went by, John became more and more sought after by journalists: 'John Lennon can always be relied upon to open his big trap and say the wrong thing,' said the top editors, 'and that sells us more newspapers.'

John's reputation for being a big mouth really took hold when the Beatles were awarded MBEs in late 1965. These special awards are given by the monarch in Britain to people who have made an outstanding contribution to public life. They may have done something good for charity or have shone in their profession in some other way. In the past many war heroes were given an MBE for bravery. And when the Beatles were given the award a number of older people were outraged.

'What have those long-haired good-for-nothings done for this country?' people moaned. John was quick to put the record straight: 'Lots of the people that complained about us receiving the MBE received theirs for heroism in war – for killing people.' Then, most shocking of all: 'We received ours for entertaining people. I'd say we deserve ours more.'

John was so unimpressed by his MBE that he gave it to his Auntie Mimi. No-nonsense Mimi was delighted with the gift, 'I always knew he was special,' she beamed as she showed the award off to her friends.

Unfortunately, by now, John's outspoken remarks had begun to make him many enemies. And in 1966 he went too far, even for many of his fans. Early that year a British newspaper had run an interview with him. John was now more vocal about politics and in this particular article he had spoken about his views on society and religion:

'Christianity will go. It will vanish and shrink,' he said. 'I'm right and I will be proved right. We're [the Beatles] more popular than Jesus right now; I don't know which will go first – rock 'n' roll or Christianity.'

At first his remarks didn't cause a reaction in Britain but, when the article was published in America, John's words were quoted out of context and a scandal broke.

'I can't believe how they have turned what I said around.' John looked glum and despairing as he shared his woes with Brian.

'That's newspaper journalists for you,' Brian replied.

'Yeah, but they're saying I said that the Beatles were

more important than Jesus. I didn't say that. And now I'm public enemy number one in America.'

'We ALL are,' answered Brian.

'They're burning our records and posters on great 'Beatle Bonfires". The situation is getting scary.' John had bags under his eyes from the sleepless nights of worrying about the situation.

'I've never felt so scared in my life,' admitted Brian. He wasn't he only one, the whole band were petrified.

'If we go on tour there, some crackpot is bound to try and kill me,' said John, who felt terrible that he had endangered the other guy's lives.

'The only way of this mess is for you to apologize,' Brian told John firmly.

At a press conference in Chicago, John made his apologies and soon afterwards the band began their fourth and final tour of the USA. By now the scenes at the concerts had become almost unreal. The band played huge stadiums and sport arenas. People needed binoculars to see them and most of the crowd couldn't hear a note for all the screaming. John, who was short-sighted and was too vain to wear glasses on stage, could see no further than his microphone. Everything was a blur.

'I'm bored of the whole thing,' moaned John.

'Look, we can do a whole show in fifteen minutes,' said Paul. It was true, the Beatles had become famous for doing short shows.

'That's fifteen minutes too long for me,' John answered.

As it turned out, the Beatles played their last live gig in the summer of 1966 at Candlestick Park in San Francisco, America. 'It was like a freak show. It wasn't about the music any more,' John told the press. 'It was time to stop.'

# CHAPTER 11

By the middle of the 1960s, the grey starchiness of the early 1950s had been replaced by a lighter, more optimistic feeling. Teenagers no longer 'put up and shut up'. Pop music, especially the Beatles, had helped them to find their own voice and most youngsters were having a great time – they weren't called the Swinging Sixties for nothing!

In 1966 a new youth movement was helping the Sixties to swing along even more. With the arrival of the hippies, it was like somebody had turned up the colour on a television set and tampered with the volume button too – everything was louder.

On their final tour of the States, John and the Beatles saw this exciting new trend for themselves. In San

Francisco young people were wearing floaty clothes in every shade of the rainbow.

'Dig the hair-dos,' said John as he watched a group of young hippies float by. It seemed that it wasn't just the girls who grew their hair – the men did, too.

'Love the flowers!' added Paul as he eyed up a pair of girls with brassy blooms tucked behind their ears.

'Mmm,' George told them. 'Apparently, we've got to make love, not war.'

'Far out,' replied Ringo, with a big grin on his face.

'Flower power', as this new trend also became known, hit its peak in the summer of 1967. As well as being about love and peace, the hippy movement was about 'dropping out' of society and living a freer life. The soundtrack for that 'Summer of Love' was the Beatles' famous album, 'Sgt. Pepper's Lonely Hearts Club Band'.

Listening to this record was like taking a trip to another world. People had never heard anything like it before. In songs like 'Lucy in the Sky With the Diamonds', John took his listeners to a fairytale land with 'marmalade skies' and girls with 'kaleidoscope eyes'. Many of the songs felt like stepping into a dream while others, such as 'With a Little Help From My Friends', tapped into the new feeling of love.

*Album cover for Sgt Pepper's Lonely Hearts Club Band*

Later that summer, the Beatles released their single 'All You Need is Love', and played the song live on the very first global satellite broadcast. Dressed in their loudest and most garish psychedelic clothes, the band now looked like full-time hippies. These days John was wearing the little round spectacles for which he became famous. The whole atmosphere around the Beatles seemed more dreamy and laid-back than it had for some time.

Part of this relaxed feeling came from the Beatles' new interests. These days they were 'into' eastern religions. It was George who first met Maharishi Mahesh Yogi, an Indian mystic, who introduced him to meditation. Before long the other Beatles became interested in the teachings of the Maharishi. They began attending lectures and practised meditation.

For John, another new obsession was taking hold, too. In the tiny, black-eyed Japanese artist called Yoko Ono, he had found the person who could be his soul mate.

After the last American tour John had been at a loose end. Without live music in his life there was an aching emptiness. As a young man he'd been interested in art, but then rock 'n' roll had taken over. Now he was older, the itch for something new was back. His search for fresh fields took him to an exhibition of Yoko's work.

As John entered the small London gallery he wasn't prepared to be quite so enchanted by the imaginative and witty pieces of work. There was something called 'Apple', which was just a plain old apple mounted on a pedestal. John was particularly taken with the 'Ceiling Painting', which invited him to climb a ladder. At the top of the ladder he used a magnifying glass to read a tiny piece of paper. There, he found a single word: 'Yes'. John thought that it was brilliant – that the journey up the ladder brought you something positive.

It was when he looked at Yoko's 'Painting to Hammer a Nail' that the first sparks flew between the couple. This work was just a blank board, a hammer and a bucket full of nails.

'May I hammer a nail in?' John asked Yoko. In truth, Yoko thought this was a cheek but she said he could if he paid her five shillings. At the time, John didn't carry money around with him.

'Well, may I hammer an imaginary nail in the painting if I give you an imaginary five shillings?' he suggested.

Immediately, Yoko felt they had connected in a special way. She liked how he'd responded to her imagination by using his own imagination. Yet, she still wasn't sure what to make of John. On the way out of the exhibition he took a big bite out of the apple on the pedestal. If he really respected her art, would he have done such a rude thing?

After that first meeting John and Yoko met many times. John was still married to Cynthia but his fascination with Yoko grew as he learned more about her amazing mind. It gradually dawned on him that they were like two halves. Best of all, Yoko showed him how to be free.

Now that the Beatles no longer toured, they didn't see Brian Epstein so much. John, who had always been closest to Brian, felt bad that he didn't see his old friend but his love of Yoko and his crumbling marriage were dominating his life.

In August 1967 the Beatles were in Wales with the Maharishi. While they were there a telephone call brought dreadful news about Brian.

'I can't believe it.' John's face drained of colour as he was told of Brian's death.

'He's been found dead in his flat in London,' he told the others. 'They've found pills.' John struggled to continue. 'They think it might be suicide.'

'No way,' said Ringo. 'I just can't believe Brian would kill himself. It must have been an accident.'

'I just wish I'd been there for him, man,' said John. 'Perhaps he needed us. All we ever thought about was how we needed Brian.'

'I'm going to miss him so much.' Paul's eyes were wide with shock.

'He was the fifth Beatle,' John said, with meaning, 'It'll never be the same again.'

For the Beatles, it never was the same again. Without Brian in charge, John and Paul began to squabble, and eventually drifted apart. John thought Paul was trying to take control of the band. Although the Beatles continued to record some of their best music, something had changed. The question was: could John and Paul weather the changes?

# CHAPTER 12

In the later years of the 1960s the Beatle who seemed to change the most was John. With his long hair, beard and his little round specs, he didn't look like the hard rock 'n' roller or the lovable mop top any more. It wasn't just his image that had been transformed, he'd altered as a person, too. He was deeper thinking and had become interested in the peace movement. He'd dabbled in acting and film-making and had published a few books.

Some of these changes came about when he fell in love with Yoko. 'The truth is that with Yoko I can see clearly for the first time,' he explained, 'There's more to life than being a Beatle and I want to try new things. The day I met Yoko is the day I left the gang,' John often said.

In late 1968 John divorced Cynthia and moved in with Yoko. 'You're joined at the hip,' moaned Paul, who was sick of Yoko being present at each and every recording session.

'I love having her around,' John reasoned. Which was an understatement because he and Yoko did EVERY-THING together.

'Look, I know that you love her but she's coming between us. It's affecting the music.'

'I'm more creative with Yoko around,' John tried to explain.

'Well, can't she just be in the background a little more?' Paul went on, but his pleas held no sway with John. Yoko and he became even more entwined and were often found whispering or giggling in the corner of the studio, much to the annoyance of the other Beatles.

If the connection between the Beatles seemed to be dying, though, the magic was still in the music. They released hit album after hit album. 'The White Album', 'Let it Be' and 'Abbey Road' all went to the top of the charts. As it happened, 'Abbey Road' was the last record that the Beatles made together.

\*\*\*

30th January 1969 was a dull grey day with a cold wind blowing. The chill in the air was matched by the coolness between the four members of the Beatles. That day they were to make their final public appearance. The last time they had played live together was in a huge muggy stadium in San Francisco. Today they were heading up to the roof top of the Apple studio in Central London where they would treat anybody who happened to be passing to their latest songs.

As the music flooded the air, girls craned their necks out of office windows to find out where it was coming from. In the streets below, stiff-looking city gents looked up, exclaiming, 'What a row!' or 'Phmmph, darn cheek!' The telephones at the recording studio started going mad as people rang up to complain or congratulate the Beatles on their performance.

Up on the roof the chill had lifted and the band was having a good time. For a few minutes all the tension between them seemed to melt away. John's voice was raw with emotion and passion. It was not to last. When the police finally broke up the act, the four men went their separate ways.

That spring, John and Yoko put on their whitest whites to become man and wife. A week later they staged their famous 'Bed-in-For-Peace' in Amsterdam. It was followed by more peace demonstrations and the release of John's first solo record, 'Give Peace a Chance'.

These days John mainly wore white. In interviews with the media he always promoted peace. At the end of the year he returned his MBE in protest against war. He wrote a brief letter to the Queen explaining his reasons – being John, he couldn't resist a little joke, too:

*Your Majesty*

*I am returning the MBE in protest against Britain's involvement in the Nigeria-Biafra thing, against our support of America in Vietnam, and against 'Cold Turkey' [John's latest single] slipping down the charts.*

*With Love,*

*John Lennon of Bag*

The Beatles carried on making music for the rest of the year but now they hardly spoke to one another. In early 1970 John finally cracked. He didn't like the way the others blamed Yoko for the rift in the band and he told them that he was quitting.

'Since I met Yoko everybody seems to think I've gone crazy,' John told Paul. ''Truth is I just fell in love, what's wrong with that?'

'That's cool,' Paul replied. 'But it's obvious your heart isn't in the Beatles any more.'

'It's with Yoko,' John went on. 'And because of that I'm leaving the Beatles.' Paul's face paled.

'It's exciting,' John tried to explain. 'It's like a new beginning for me.' But Paul didn't see it that way. He was heart-broken.

The public did not hear about the Beatles' split until

April, when Paul McCartney issued a press release that he was leaving the band. In the past it was John who had always done the talking. It was many years before he forgave Paul for going public about the band's break-up first. Especially because *he* claimed to be leaving the band when John had already done so.

The Beatles were the most popular band on the planet and the news of their break-up hit many fans like a death in the family. There was shock, sadness, disbelief and anger – there were even tears. The Beatles had helped to put the 'swing' into the Sixties, what would the 1970s be like without them? John, who had just enough of Mimi's 'no-nonsense' attitude to keep him sane, had already moved on: 'It's not a great disaster,' he told them. 'People keep talking about it as if it's the end of the earth. It's only a rock group that split up. It's nothing important.'

# CHAPTER 13

At the end of the 1960s John and Yoko bought a beautiful white mansion near Ascot in England. 'It's like a house from a romantic novel,' said John. After the band split, the starry-eyed couple retreated there to make a new beginning.

As a young boy, and as a teenager, John had dreamed of fame and making pots of money. Now, he was a millionaire many times over and he cherished the quiet life. Most of all, he enjoyed being alone with Yoko. As the sun set over the tranquil gardens of their new home, John and Yoko were often seen walking along holding hands. At these times, they seemed lost in their own little world.

Over the years John tapped into different sides of his

creativity but music always remained his first love. At the end of 1970 John and Yoko released the 'John Lennon/Plastic Ono Band' album. 'John has a strong social message,' said a review in the music press, 'while at the same time, he gets to grip with his own past and present.' In his song, 'Working Class Hero', John was angry about people being treated badly because of their class. In 'Love', a quiet piano accompanied his gentle voice as he told us what love is. Most painful of all, was his song 'Mother', in which he mourned the loss of his own mother all those years ago. 'Nobody has heard John sound so honest and raw,' the music reviewer continued.

The following year John sat down at a white piano in a white room of the white mansion where he lived. As he began playing a simple melody he started singing what would become his most famous lyrics. The song was called 'Imagine' and John was asking people to imagine a world where people lived in peace. A place where nobody suffered or starved and where people lived together as a 'brotherhood of man'.

The words to the song had come to him when he was flying in a plane and he'd jotted them down quickly on the back of a hotel bill. 'It's just "Working Class Hero" with chocolate on,' laughed John but the song has come to mean so much more.

As John performed the song, Yoko glided across the room, her long, white dress trailing, as she moved gently from window to window, opening the shutters and letting in the light. This magical scene was captured on camera and it was shown on television when the single was in the charts.

Just as the song has become so popular, the image of John and Yoko in their white room has become etched on people's minds. 'Imagine' went on to become a massive hit throughout the world. Over 30 years later it was voted the best song of the 20th century.

# CHAPTER 14

The next chapter of John and Yoko's life was as far removed from the English countryside as can be. In September 1972, they packed up their bags to fly to America where they settled in the bustling city of New York. By now John was ready to escape Britain where he felt that people just remembered him as one of the Beatles.

'In New York, I can walk or cycle around without being hassled by fans,' he explained, his eyes alive with excitement. 'I'm also taken seriously as an artist.'

As usual, Yoko was at his side. She had her own reasons for wanting to be in New York: 'I know the city well because I've spent a lot of time here,' she told reporters. 'This is where I'd like John and I have to our child.' Yoko wasn't pregnant but it was no secret that the couple yearned for children.

For John moving to America was like another new beginning. Needless to say, Auntie Mimi had her say, too: 'John, don't get taken in by those awful Americans and come back soon.'

As it happened, John never returned to Britain. He loved the freedom of living in New York. His first few years were spent experimenting with music, finding different ways of promoting peace and discovering new political causes in which to become involved.

Soon after arriving in the States, the single 'Happy Xmas, War is Over' was released, becoming another anthem for the peace movement. In the following years the music seemed to pour out of John. He released album after album, including 'Some Time in New York City', 'Mind Games', 'Walls and Bridges', 'Rock 'n' Roll' and 'Shaved Fish'.

While every album wasn't quite a winner, John's fans always supported their hero. He still conjured up the odd masterpiece and these days he performed with a kind of soul that nobody had seen even when he was a Beatle. Nowhere did his passion shine more than when he was on stage. In those years John performed some of the best live music of his lifetime.

John got on with making music but he was never the kind of person to stay quiet for long. During these years John and Yoko spoke out against the bombing of Vietnam by America and spoke up for the civil rights movement. They also played a series of live gigs to raise money for charity, sometimes for children, otherwise for political causes close to their hearts.

John's political views were beginning to catch up with him, though. He desperately wanted a green card so he could live and work in America for good. But it turned out that the men at the Federal Bureau of Investigation (FBI) had opened a file on him in the 1960s; and by 1972 it was bulging. It included a list of his political movements, as well as his involvement in drugs. The FBI were scared that John was so popular with American youth that he had the power to stir up anti-establishment feeling: 'This guy could lead our teenagers to revolution,' said one of the fed agents. 'England can keep him. We gotta find a way to get him deported.' The FBI tried very hard to catch John out:

'Every time I pick up the phone there's a weird buzzing noise,' John told Yoko, 'they must be bugging me.'

When John played live there were often FBI men in the audience:

'Did you hear that Bud?' said the fed agent standing at the back of the Lennon concert. 'He just said: "Woman is the nigger of the world," ...sounds bad to me.'

After three long years of trying to get John deported, however, the FBI couldn't pin anything on him and in 1975 an order for his deportation was finally dropped. The very next day, 9 October, John and Yoko had their first child together, a longed for son they named Sean Ono Lennon.

'I can't believe he has the same birthday as me,' beamed John as he stroked a lock of black hair on the little boy's forehead.

'Believe and it can happen,' answered Yoko who cuddled their precious little bundle.

'This is a second chance for me,' said John, 'this time I'm going to be a good father.'

John was true to his word. Not being around for his son Julian had haunted him and with Sean he was determined to be there every step of the way. Nobody could quite believe it when John Lennon, founder of the Beatles and wild man of rock 'n' roll, put down his guitar and became a house-husband for the next five years of his life.

The men at the FBI couldn't believe it either:

'Have you heard Bud… that Lennon guy is baking his own bread and stays home to look after the baby?'

'Gee, well that should keep him out of trouble for a while.'

# CHAPTER 15

'Life begins at forty, Mimi,' John joked with his Auntie. The year was 1980 and John and Yoko were still living in New York. John, who turned forty that year, regularly spoke with his auntie on the telephone. No-nonsense Mimi still lived in the bungalow by the sea that John had bought for her in Poole, Dorset. Even though she was in her late seventies Mimi liked a chuckle at some of the new and more outrageous British comedies on television.

'Oh our John, this new show doesn't half make me laugh!'

'Send us a tape over then,' John asked. 'Sean and I still love *Fawlty Towers* and the Monty Python stuff you sent over is always a hoot.'

'How is that little boy? I hope you're not still spoiling him.'

'Spoiling him rotten Auntie,' John admitted. He and Yoko had decided that if Sean were to grow up like John then he'd want things because he hadn't had them. Whereas if he had EVERYTHING from an early age then eventually he wouldn't want anything. The experiment seemed to be working.

'Actually Auntie,' John went on, 'Sean's most treasured possession is his collection of rocks.'

'Good job it isn't rocks and roll,' joked Mimi.

'You have to admit that rock 'n' roll was a good career for me, Auntie.'

'Mmm, well you haven't done much lately. Perhaps you've grown out of all that nonsense.' Mimi hoped he'd stick to writing or something more respectable.

'Ah well, this is going to be a big year for me. I've been writing songs again and I'm gonna release an album.'

Mimi was silent – a Mimi silence said more than words ever could.

'Who knows I might even make it back home for a tour.' Though John loved America, part of him pined for Britain and that year he began planning a world tour, taking in his hometown of Liverpool. Mimi thrilled at the idea of seeing her wayward nephew once again.

Over the past five years, far away from the prying eyes of the press, John had been busy. Not only was he a devoted dad to Sean but he'd enjoyed travelling, especially to South Africa and Bermuda. He'd also healed the rift with his eldest son, Julian, who now came over to the States during his school holidays. Julian had inherited his father's looks and his passion for music. Some of their best times together were spent playing the guitar or listening to records.

During this time John had made friends with the other Beatles, too. Paul and his wife Linda often dropped in on John and Yoko at their huge sprawling apartment in New York. Sometimes the old friends jammed together. But, as they sat around chatting about the past and talking about their families, there was never any talk of them actually making a comeback together.

For John, the high point of 1980 was returning to the recording studio. He'd missed making music – the emptiness was like an ache that refused to go away. Brimming with childlike enthusiasm, he and Yoko made an album called 'Double Fantasy'. Gone was the angry John of yesteryear. In his place was a man who felt content and happy with his lot in life. In 'Starting Over', he sounded on top of the world, celebrating his love for Yoko and his delight to be back making music. On 'Beautiful Boy' he sang of his love for his son Sean. And, in 'Watching the Wheels' he seemed to have found an inner peace. These days he could watch the world go by without getting angry at what he saw.

'Double Fantasy' was received with mixed reviews but people were mostly happy that John was on the scene again. Meanwhile, John and Yoko were excited at being back in the limelight. True, being in the public eye meant attending more interviews with the press. It also meant more trips to the music studio. But John was enjoying himself and he was feeling relaxed.

Though they were chauffeur driven most places John and Yoko thought nothing of walking a few blocks home to their apartment. They never really questioned how safe this was and they often stopped to sign autographs for the fans. Little did they know that a young man called Mark Chapman had been watching their comings and goings for weeks. And that there was something strange and unsettling about the way his eyes followed John.

Since the release of 'Double Fantasy', John had been on top form in his interviews with the press. He was as outspoken as ever, especially when he was on the subject of peace: 'Mahatma Gandhi and Martin Luther King are great examples of fantastic non-violents who died violently,' he told one journalist. 'I can never work that out. We're pacifists, but I'm not sure what it means when you're such a pacifist that you get shot. I can never understand that.' Those very words would later haunt many of his fans. It was as if he had predicted that something terrible was about to happen.

On Monday, 8 December 1980, John and Yoko left for the recording studio in the afternoon. As they stepped out of their apartment block, John was whistling. Outside they bumped straight into a fan who asked John to sign his copy of 'Double Fantasy'. This 'fan' was Mark Chapman and as their eyes met John felt something was out of place: 'Is that all?' he asked the man, 'Do you want anything else?' As the man shuffled off John turned to Yoko: 'I know New York is full of weirdos but that guy really gave me the creeps.'

'Me, too,' Yoko agreed but they were used to strange characters pestering them.

John and Yoko returned home at 10.49pm. As they walked the short distance to the lobby of the apartment block a voice called out of the darkness. 'Mr Lennon?'

John's eyes squinted as he peered into the shadows. Standing there was Mark Chapman and in his hand was a revolver. Suddenly, five shots were fired. The bullets entered John's arms and back. As he staggered towards the lobby, he groaned, 'I'm shot, I'm shot.'

These were the last words spoken by John Lennon. As Yoko's screams filled the humid night air, John was being bundled into the back of a police car. By the time he arrived at hospital, he had lost a lot of blood. He was pronounced dead at 11.07pm.

All around the world people were shocked to hear the terrible news of John's murder. They couldn't believe they'd never hear John again. The passionate rock 'n' roller with the gut-wrenching voice was gone. The outspoken Beatle who often got in trouble for saying the wrong thing was silenced. And, with his death the world had lost one of its greatest champions of peace.

Over the following days and weeks people gathered in major cities to remember John. In his hometown of Liverpool, 25,000 people flooded into the city centre to honour their hero. Radio stations everywhere paid tribute by playing his records over and over.

In her house by the sea, Auntie Mimi quietly remembered the man with whom she'd shared so many ups and downs. The photograph of John was back on the mantelpiece. 'I always took it down when he was naughty,' she explained to one of her friends. 'Then, when we were back on speaking terms I'd put it back up. He didn't stop being naughty in one way or another until the day he died,' she went on. 'Now that he's gone I shall always keep his photograph there.' With that the tears that had been welling in her eyes began to fall.

On December 14th, the day of John's cremation, Yoko released a statement for John's fans: 'Bless you for your tears and prayers. I saw John smiling in the sky. I saw sorrow changing into clarity. I saw all of us becoming one mind. Thank you. Love, Yoko'. These were difficult and dark days for Yoko. She spent most of her time alone. 'He's still beside me,' she told friends. 'John is still around.'

When the Beatles split, John had told his fans to take solace in the music: 'When you want to remember us you still have the records to play,' he reasoned. John has left behind some of the most popular and loved pop music ever, but he is still dearly missed. And it isn't just his fans that feel his loss.

In an uncertain world, where peace seems so fragile, we need people who will get up and speak out against war. In losing John Lennon, we have lost one of the most charismatic and imaginative campaigners for the peace movement.

# Quiz

*After you've finished the book, test yourself and see how well you remember what you've read.*

**1. When John Lennon was born in 1940 his father, Freddy, was:**
Down the pub
Away at sea
Putting up a bomb shelter in the backyard

**2. John's first years were spent in an area of Liverpool known as:**
Coin Street
Shilling Market
Penny Lane

**3. As a child, John's favourite pastime was:**
Reading books in his bedroom
Playing golf with his Uncle George
Singing with the church choir

**4. In 1955, Bill Haley and the Comets released a popular film called:**
Hickory Dickory Rock
Chock-a-block Rock
Rock Around the Clock

**5. John's mother, Julia, encouraged his interest in music by:**
Buying him a tambourine for his ninth birthday
Showing him how to play chords on her banjo
Taking him to the opera every month

**6. Paul McCartney's father thought John was:**
A bad influence who stopped his son doing his schoolwork
A talented musician with a great future
A greedy slob who ate everything in the house when he came round

**7. John met his first wife, Cynthia:**
In a lettering class at art college
Through a friend of his Aunt Mimi
At a trendy new milkbar

**8. The original name for John, Paul and George's band was:**
The Gravediggers
The Quarry Men
The Rocking Miners

**9. The Beatles' first big break in Hamburg came to a sudden end when:**
Their instruments were stolen by fans
John fell off the stage and broke both legs
It was found they did not have permits to work in Germany

**10. When he became manager, Brian Epstein insisted that the group:**
Get their hair cut
Go on the Atkins diet
Brush their teeth before performances

**11. The Beatles' first Number 1 hit was:**
Love Me Do
Please, Please Me
She Loves You

**12. When the Beatles performed in America, fans would throw at the stage:**
Sherbet lemons
Gobstoppers
Jelly beans

**13. John Lennon had his Rolls Royce painted in:**
Rainbow colours
Psychedelic patterns
Black and white spots

**14. In 1966 John caused much offence by claiming the Beatles were more popular than:**
Jesus
Elvis
The Queen

**15. George Harrison introduced the rest of the Beatles to:**
The Chinese hypnotist, Fu Manchu
The Indian mystic, Maharishi Mahesh Yogi
The Australian kangaroo-breeder, Bruce Douglas

**16. When John saw Yoko Ono's artwork 'Apple' on its pedestal he:**
Took a bite out of it and put it back
Swapped it for an orange
Put it in his pocket and walked off with it

**17. During their honeymoon John and Yoko:**
Gave away £1 million to the RSPCA
Stayed in bed as a protest against war and violence
Swam the English Channel to raise funds for charity

**18. John Lennon's most famous song is:**
Dream
Believe
Imagine

**19. When John and Yoko moved to New York, the FBI:**
Provided them with an armed escort
Bugged their phones
Asked them to become secret agents

**20. Before he died, John Lennon encouraged people to remember the Beatles by:**
Playing their records
Visiting Penny Lane
Joining the official fan club

# Key dates

1940 – John is born in Liverpool

1944 – John's parents split up and he is sent to live with his Aunt Mimi.

1956 – Elvis Presley's *Heartbreak Hotel* goes to No 1 in the pop charts. John has found a hero.

1957 – John meets Paul McCartney, and invites him to join his band, the Quarry Men.

1958 – John's mother, Julia, is killed in an accident.

1959 – The Quarry Men change their name to the Beatles, and go on tour in Germany.

1961 – Brian Epstein becomes the Beatles' manager.

1962 – Stuart Sutcliffe, band member and John's great friend, dies in Hamburg. Ringo Starr replaces Pete Best as drummer in the band. In August John marries his girlfriend Cynthia in Liverpool. The Beatles' single 'Love me do' is released and becomes an immediate hit.

1963 – John and Cynthia's son Julian is born. The Beatles enjoy a string of No 1 hits.

1964 – Beatlemania spreads across the world.

1965 – The Beatles are awarded the MBE. John feels increasingly unhappy with fame.

1966 – The Beatles' album Sergeant Pepper's Lonely Hearts Club Band becomes the sound of the summer.

1968 – John divorces Cynthia and moves in with Yoko Ono. Tension builds between John and the band.

1969 – The Beatles make their final public appearance on the roof top of the Apple studio in London. John and Yoko get married and do their famous seven-day 'Bed-in for Peace'.

1970 – John quits the Beatles and launches his solo career.

1972 – John and Yoko move to New York.

1975 – Sean Ono Lennon is born.

1980 – John is shot by Mark Chapman outside his New York apartment.

A former music journalist, Liz Gogerly now writes children's books. Among her most popular titles are biographies on Elvis Presley (Hodder Wayland), Hitler and Sigmund Freud (Watts). She lives in Brighton and has a young son.